Sky the Oar

Sky the Oar

Poems

PAGE 63 IS FOR US ALL.

Stacy R. Nigliazzo

9.21.18

Press 53
Winston-Salem

Press 53, LLC
PO Box 30314
Winston-Salem, NC 27130

First Edition

A TOM LOMBARDO POETRY SELECTION

Cover design by Kevin Morgan Watson

Author photo by Angi Lewis Photography
www.angilewis.com

Library of Congress Control Number
2018951829

Printed on acid-free paper
ISBN 978-1-941209-86-8

for Lindsey Nicole Eastridge

Acknowledgments

My sincerest appreciation to the editors of the journals in which these poems first appeared, often in earlier versions:

American Journal of Nursing: "Cavitation"

As It Ought To Be Saturday Poetry Series: "Aria," "Cloudburst," "Ploughshare"

Beloit Poetry Journal: "Nocturne"

CityLitRag: "Biopsy," "Harvest Crescent"

Diverse-City (Austin International Poetry Festival): "Ad Patres"

Eunoia Review: "An Unlatched Square," "Art," "How He Told Police He Found Her"

Grit, Gravity & Grace (The College of Physicians of Philadelphia): "Ophelia"

Houseboat: "I am," "The day he stopped breathing, I," "What His Family Says"

Ilanot Review: "Sky the Oar"

Italian Americana: "Song"

The Journal of Compressed Creative Arts (Matter Press): "Harvesting Her Heart"

Lumen: "Triptych"

One: "Healthcare Exchange"

Ovunque Siamo: "Convulsion," "Dusk," "Prophet"

Queen of Cups: "The New Courthouse, Built from the Old Cathedral"

Right Hand Pointing (One Sentence Poems): "Gunwale," "Mountain Fold," "Petal Fold"

Rockvale Review: "Finding the Desert at Daybreak"

Snapdragon: "Postern"

Wyvern Lit: "A Tiding of Magpies," "Because the eyelet," "Hemoptysis," "When her lines went flat"

Yellow Chair Review: "Talisman/Lunatic"

Warmest gratitude to my editor Tom Lombardo and my publisher Kevin Morgan Watson of Press 53 for their faith in me, to Gabrielle Langley for her artist's insight, and to Chris, Lola, and Zoe for their patience and love.

Contents

I

II

III

IV

I

River

I have never burned   white

       in the sick room.

              I do not silence my hair with a cap.

I pour,

    water   over rock,

          black as pitch.

              The matchstick moon in my pocket.

Poetry

Ink stirs my right atrium

     breaching the latch—

                      obsidian   blue.

I am

Mary Magdalene

          anointing the feet of an inmate with fennel and thyme,

a black birch cradling an infant   flung

                            from a three-story window.

Nocturne

Evening breaks kindly,

       without bruise   or blow.

Owling air,

        black bowl,   wreath of fireflies.

*

I wash his hands and face with castile soap,

     bear up

        my greenstick heart.

    Wait for his parents   who don't yet know

his new moon stare—

   small boy,

     a dim road,

         his face   in the black water.

His eyes,   I can't close.

Song

Lavender oil,   mercury glass,

          Morphine.

He is a setting   star—

               what else

          can I bring—a flask of lapsang—

                              blood in a soup?

The hair from his pillow,

          a song.

His mother's bedside chair

bore a groove in the floor.

                            On the eleventh day,

                    when the tube was pulled out—

                                            he woke—

beryl eyes

            brimming light,

                                    a covey of clouds.

How He Told Police He Found Her

She was   *broken*

when I found her,

bloody handprints across the vomit-soaked floor—

from the bathroom   *to the bedroom—*

when I found her—

sitting quietly in a well of blood—

after she asked a colleague to cover her shift for the next day—

"I can't live   this way..."

after our boys fell asleep behind a locked door—

when I found her   *I called police—*

blew up pictures from our wedding day for the easel at the chapel—

when I found her—

Biopsy

Radiation   raised the ground.

                    She drank a glass of rainwater.

                                      Rousing   seeds.

The incision was made—

          petals

                  broke

              beneath the blade—

                                          a clutch of tulips.

Ploughshare

Where is she?

Her brain,

lost—

lungs rise and set,

a plastic sky.

Those who love her

cradling   her warm hands.

Unlatched Square

Cold cloths for fever,

        salt for his throat—   railing heart.

I hold out my hand,   tuck his hair behind one ear—

        Death   is here,

        beneath a scrap quilt,

        needling

        an unlatched square—

in the far corner—

        nestled in my collarbone,

        its beak

        in my hair—

Because the eyelet

      ripped clean,

        I slipped off my dress, tore a seam   in my hip,

crept into the river,

          unraveled—

                    I have no edge.

The day he stopped breathing, I

covered him in warm blankets,

       held his mother's hand—

          collected his blood—

   air and bone,

        a lambent screen—

    sterile procedures,   a fetid room—

his mother's hand,

   warm blankets.

Offering

The surgeon reads aloud, before the first cut

Jack,

thirty-five years old

with three sons,

loves fly fishing.

He's giving three people his lungs and his eyes.

II

Cloudburst

She struck the windshield,

                    stars unpinned—

                                        silver glass.

Penumbrae

I draped my palm over her chest,

        her father   wept—

                Did she die?

Thrum of light,

    her little brother on the family room floor,

                folding cranes.

Mountain Fold

We culled the nettle from her lung—

she flew—

red kite rowing a pleat of light,

unthreaded eye—

Dusk

Papers permit natural death.

      I read aloud words underlined in red from *The Hiding Place*.

Her lungs won't last the day—

      each breath,   a prayer,

          rose water of my chest

                cleaved from her own skin.

      A golden pitcher   tips to earth,

        empty,

              it sets.

Leaving

She

    was   *leaving*

            him.

                     The cracked hinge,
                fractured pane

                over the bedpost.

White-crowned sparrow on the barrel bolt latch,

        hollow-boned,

                white-winged.

White Window

He was found along the highway,

        thrown   from his motorcycle

                into the mouth of a culvert.

    He'd followed her through six states   eight restraining orders.

In the intensive care ward,

    an armed guard rests his palm against the white pane—

             ice like splintered glass,

          green blades,

                    blood moon.

Cavitation

We speak plainly,   softly,

     as we are taught.

Her next of kin,

     last *recently dialed* contact.

             In this room,

     dead walls—a clicking   clock.

*

What if it hadn't rained?

     If she hadn't worked late?

     If the lidless sky hadn't plucked out the sun?

Requiem for a Twenty-Six-Year-Old Holding His
Son for the Last Time

The inkwell fell on its side   at the tap of a fingernail,

        spilling into the sun.

The stars bled through

            his infant son across the bedside rail,

                hallowed bread.

Frequently Asked Questions by My Patients

1.

Who are you?

2.

Who am   I?

3.

Will you stay?

When her lines went flat

she came untethered;

    milkweed skin,

        a salt-stained sky.

    We tend like tailors   tying tiny knots.

Listen—

    the moon,

        a rusted nail through an iron gate.

Harvesting Her Heart

And when the surgeon pierced her breastbone—   quickening

                        light—

                        scatter of fireflies.

Talisman

I carry   pieces of the Malbec sky,

              scattering salt to stay the witches—

                           shivering the stars into dust.

III

Aria

The librettist

                paints the air,

      pleading

                    the ink-raked light—

                          Aprimi il petto e vedrai scritto in core.

After the stroke he could not   speak,

                        but he could sing Caccini—

Ophelia

She'd lost her breasts,

      pieces of her   liver,

           spleen—

      but was glad to have blood drawn

in the north tower,

      when the cellist played;

                    the rosewood bridge,   polished ribs,

                                a carved neck,

                        wire-wound strings

                                  tuned in perfect fifths—

Say It

Unnamed woman fatally stabbed, police investigating...

Crown of larkspur.   Starless

                    sky   and its pail of warm milk.

A lantern light I turn, and turn.

                    Her name—

                                        Lindsey.

Triptych

I.

Texas firefighter kills girlfriend and then himself as she prepared to leave abusive relationship: report

BY NICOLE HENSLEY / NEW YORK DAILY NEWS/ Published: Friday, May 22, 2015, 4:06 PM/ Updated: Friday, May 22, 2015, 4:06 PM

Family of a Houston, **Texas nurse knew something was wrong** when she failed to pick up her young daughter from school.

Those fears were not unfounded — knowing she'd soon be leaving her abusive firefighter boyfriend — and led to the gruesome discovery of Caroline Minjares, 36, dead in her home. They also found her boyfriend, dead by taking his own life on Thursday night.

"She told me 'if he ever left her, he was going to kill her.' That's pretty much what ended up happening," Minjares' brother, Eduardo Minjares told KHOU-TV.

A Houston firefighter is believed to have killed his girlfriend, Caroline Minjares, pictured, on before taking his own life at her home.

It's believed Richard Deluna, a 40-year-old firefighter with Houston Fire Department, broke into Minjares' home as **she** slept after a nursing shift, stabbed her to death and then stuck around for several hours until the victim's mother called, authorities said.

He claimed to be at work, Deluna told the worried mother, but really, he was at Minjares' home as **she** lay dead. He then killed himself, authorities added.

Shortly after the phone call, Minjares' relatives burst into the home screaming **'where is she'** before finding the bodies, neighbors told KPRC-TV.

"He's just a coward I don't know why he did this to our family," Eduardo Minjares added. "Our family is devastated."

Minjares and Deluna had been dating for about one year and had recently decided she would end their relationship, KHOU-TV reported.

A statement from Houston Professional Fire Fighters Association made no reference to the circumstances of Deluna's death, but said local firefighters were in mourning over the off-duty death.

"Our organization will strive to help support his brothers and sisters in the fire service, his family and his friends in this difficult time. Please keep his family and friends in your thoughts and prayers as answers are sought after this inexplicable tragedy," fire officials wrote to KPRC-TV.

Minjares, a nurse at Neighbors Emergency Center, leaves behind two daughters, ages 5 and 14.

Ad Patres

for Bob C. Jones, MD

I imagine

                the feathery wood

        long after the procession;

                            the blue oak,

        his ashes,

                                      hyacinths.

Petal Fold

The surgeon knows all the parts of the brain but he does not know his patient's dreams.
—Richard Selzer

A closed fist   of lung;

the woman on the table ahead of an aperture.

*

The blade   steps

through the door of her breastbone;

paper wings,

the splayed ribs of a pine boat.

In the Garden

He sips black tea on a stone bench.

                    The buckled sycamore,   its many hands

          red-veined on the cold ground.

Three Patients on Easter Sunday

A man who slipped and fell in a liter of his own blood

                after three days of rye whiskey.

A three-week-old,

          liseran   in a pillowcase.

A woman with silver eyes,

      skin like paper birch leaves,

               whose feet never touched the ground.

Gunwale

The water   wakes—

      creeps

            into the crawl space—

                    anchor

         the floor,

                        closed fist on the siderail—

Art

I worry my hands   across the spire of your breastbone,

    catch a flicker—

               breath.

*

Blue hearts,   red sunflowers,

       the handprints of your children.

Prophet

You may surrender your baby at any hospital in Texas without fear of punishment...
—Safe Haven Law

She held him,

    curled beneath her rib,

as he pushed through water   for air,

          handed him across the desk—

        heavy,

               her   howling arms.

Moses split the Red Sea,

    born of a bulrush womb in the Nile River—

        the black cord   still woven in his belly.

A Tiding of Magpies

We carry needles full of sleep—

     hoarding everything shiny and sharp

  so she can't hurt herself.

          She split

              the air—

     cackling

                      birdshot—

because the hackberry is bleeding

    and spider wasps are scratching into the sun—

Triptych

II.

Texas firefighter kills girlfriend and then himself as she prepared to leave abusive relationship: report

BY NICOLE HENSLEY / NEW YORK DAILY NEWS/ Published: Friday, May 22, 2015, 4:06 PM/ Updated: Friday, May 22, 2015, 4:06 PM

Family of a Houston, Texas nurse knew something was wrong when she failed to pick up her young daughter from school.

Those fears were not unfounded — knowing she'd soon be leaving her abusive **firefighter** boyfriend — and led to the gruesome discovery of Caroline Minjares, 36, dead in **her** home. They also found her **boyfriend,** dead by taking his own life on Thursday night.

"She told me 'if **he** ever left her, **he** was going to kill her.' That's pretty much what ended up happening," Minjares' brother, Eduardo Minjares told KHOU-TV.

A Houston **firefighter** is believed to have **killed his girlfriend**, Caroline Minjares, pictured, on **before taking his own life** at her home.

It's believed Richard Deluna, **a** 40-year-old **firefighter** with Houston Fire Department, broke into Minjares' home as she slept after a nursing shift, **stabbed her to death** and then stuck around for several hours until the victim's mother called, authorities said.

He **claimed to be at work,** Deluna told the worried mother, but really, he **was** at Minjares' **home as she lay dead.** He then **killed himself**, authorities added.

Shortly after the phone call, Minjares' relatives burst into the home screaming 'where is she' before finding the bodies, neighbors told KPRC-TV.

"He's just a coward I don't know why he did this to our family," Eduardo Minjares added. "Our family is devastated."

Minjares and Deluna had been dating for about one year and had recently decided she would end their relationship, KHOU-TV reported.

A statement from **Houston Professional Fire Fighters Association** made no reference to the circumstances of Deluna's death, but said local firefighters were in mourning over the off-duty death.

"Our organization will strive to help support his brothers and sisters in the fire service, his family and his friends in this difficult time. **Please keep his family and friends in your thoughts and prayers** as answers are sought after this inexplicable tragedy," fire officials wrote to KPRC-TV.

Minjares, a nurse at Neighbors Emergency Center, leaves behind two daughters, ages 5 and 14.

IV

Postern

I watch her fall

                away.

Starched white,

                        red phlox pressed in a book.

Healthcare Exchange

He crooks his brow,

    the pad from his white coat,

            a remedy   I can't afford—

    rinses his hands—

           nettle moths slip through the faucet.

The meter rolls,

    blackbirds preen in oil and water.

Practice

We practiced how he'd count them

        after the biopsy,

                    the pink seconds beneath a fingernail

            pressed and released—

            rustling

                  deep

         as the marrow of the milk moon—

                        I let him use my hands.

Chord

Here rests the heart of Frédéric Chopin...
—Warsaw, Poland

Blood cognac,

sternum   of sky,

stone pillar at the Holy Cross Church.

The oaring of the human heart.

On the third day

I fill the well with oil,

                    listen;

                the wick of your eyes.

*

Drum of rain.

                    Iris   of the lake.

Vespers

We stand together   on the bank,

      slip into the laden arms of the dark water.

Marigold,   milkweed,

           all that is left of the light.

                  The cellar of the lake.

What His Family Says

Please,   *leave the door open.*

   It feels like an animal is clawing through my chest.

                    Mother of God—

   my son can't be dead,

                    I just washed and braided his hair—

The New Courthouse Built from the Old Cathedral

Stained glass   stripped pale as bone,

          a cluster of pews with carved backs,

a mahogany bench sheltering the fingernail of a martyred saint,

                    and the blessed sacristy.

Hemoptysis

He clamors into the waiting room,

       left lung in a dinner napkin.

             Coughing for two weeks—just spit blood.

I am a steward of viscera.

        I gather it up,   listen

                    with my stethoscope.

He pays the clerk   a scrap of liver,

       three fingernails.

Finding the Desert at Daybreak

Summer rain and creosote.

        In the book of your eyes,

    silver clouds   casting skins over red rock,

                        the sun on a feather grass leaf.

Triptych

III.

Texas firefighter kills girlfriend and then himself as she prepared to leave abusive relationship: report

BY NICOLE HENSLEY / NEW YORK DAILY NEWS/ Published: Friday, May 22, 2015, 4:06 PM/ Updated: Friday, May 22, 2015, 4:06 PM

Family of a Houston, Texas nurse knew something was wrong when she failed to pick up her young daughter from school.

Those fears were not unfounded — **know**ing she'd soon be leaving her abusive firefighter boyfriend — and led to the gruesome discovery of Caroline Minjares, 36, dead in her home. They also found her boyfriend, dead by taking his own life on Thursday night.

"She told me 'if he ever left her, he was going to kill her.' That's pretty much what ended up happening," Minjares' brother, Eduardo Minjares told KHOU-TV.

A Houston firefighter is believed to have killed his girlfriend, Caroline Minjares, pictured, on before taking his own life at her home.

It's believed Richard Deluna, a 40-year-old firefighter with Houston Fire Department, broke into Minjares' home as she slept after a nursing shift, stabbed her to death and then stuck around for several hours until the victim's mother called, authorities said.

He claimed to be at work, Deluna told the worried mother, **but** really, he **w**as at Minjar**e**s' home as she lay dead. He then killed himself, authorities added.

Shortly after the phone call, Minjares' relatives burst into the home screaming 'where is she' before finding the bodies, neighbors told KPRC-TV.

"He's just a coward I **don't** know why he did this to our family," Eduardo Minjares added. "Our family is devastated."

Minjares and Deluna had been dating for about one year and had recently decided she would end their relationship, KHOU-TV reported.

A statement from Houston Professional Fire Fighters Association made no reference to the circumstances of Deluna's death, but said local firefighters were in mourning over the off-duty death.

"Our organization will strive to help support his brothers and sisters in the fire service, his family and his friends in this difficult time. Please keep his family and friends in your thoughts and prayers as answers are sought after this inexplicable tragedy," fire officials wrote to KPRC-TV.

Minjares, a nurse at Neighbors Emergency Center, leaves behind two daughters, ages 5 and 14.

Speak

No one saw   or heard.

      Don't tell anyone—

                                    tell everyone.

Sky the Oar

She was

        and will again be

   the coxswain at stern;   whitewater,

        the climbing curve of her collarbone.

Lent

The chaplain blesses my hands;

wine and bread,

ashes.

Notes

"Ad Patres"

This poem was written in memory of Bob Clarence Jones, MD of Madisonville, Texas, who died peacefully at his home on July 23, 2014. The finest physician and the dearest man I've ever known.

"Aria"

This poem references a line from the song "Amarilli, Mia Bella," composed in 1601 (or earlier) by Giulio Caccini.

"Chord"

This poem was written to honor Frédéric Chopin, who died in October of 1849 in France. It was reportedly his wish that his heart be buried in his native Poland after his death. His eldest sister, Ludwika Jêdrzejewicz, is said to have facilitated the removal of Chopin's heart from his body after he died, smuggling it back to Poland in a jar of cognac. It is now buried inside a stone pillar at the Holy Cross Church in Warsaw. (https:/ /www.newyorker.com/culture/culture-desk/chopins-heart).

"Cloudburst," "Harvesting Her Heart," & "Ploughshare"

These poems were written for Stephanie Alexandra Vafiadis of Houston, Texas, a dear friend and colleague who was killed in a car accident on August 15, 2016.

"Leaving," "Triptych I, II, & III"

These poems were written for Caroline Minjares of Houston, Texas, a friend and colleague who was killed by her intimate partner on May 21, 2015.

"Mountain Fold"

A fundamental origami fold. The paper is folded in half with the crease at the top.

"Petal Fold"

An intermediate origami fold. The paper is folded to transform a square base into a boat shape, constituting the body of crane. The epigraph for this poem was taken from the book *Mortal Lessons* by Richard Selzer.

"Prophet"

This poem was written in recognition of the Texas Safe Haven Law, also referred to as the Baby Moses Law. It allows a parent to legally surrender custody of an infant (up to sixty days old) to any hospital, fire house, or police station without repercussions.

"Say It"

This poem was written for Lindsey Nicole Eastridge of Mesa, Arizona, to whom this book is dedicated. Beloved mother, daughter, wife, sister, niece, and friend, she was killed by a stranger in a random act of violence on February 2, 2018.

Stacy R. Nigliazzo is the award-winning author of *Scissored Moon* (Press 53, 2013). Her poems have appeared in numerous journals and anthologies including the *American Journal of Nursing*, *Bellevue Literary Review*, *Beloit Poetry Journal*, *Ilanot Review*, and the *Journal of the American Medical Association*. She is co-editor of the anthology *Red Sky, Poetry on the Global Epidemic of Violence Against Women*. She lives in Houston, Texas, and has worked as an emergency room nurse for the past twelve years.